Bridgeport Then and Now

A collection of photos that takes us through
the changes of time
in the "Old Neighborhood"

———————

John McKenzie

Bridgeport Then and Now

Copyright © 2015 by John McKenzie

All Rights Reserved

ISBN: 13: 978-1519476913

PREFACE

Another Bridgeport book ...really? Why? Because I want to! And besides, these books are nice fundraisers. Actually, there is another reason for this book... So many times as I drive or walk around Bridgeport I say to myself, "I wonder what used to be there?" I have also listened to people talk about places way back when and I have wondered, "Where was that exactly?" Also, people who no longer live in the area have asked, "Is such and such a place still there?" So....I decided to do another book that would show Bridgeport BEFORE and AFTER photos.

I think this is a fun book that will bring back memories. However, what fascinates me is how the Bridgeport community is always evolving, always changing and yet this community continues to permeate with life and energy. Old business are gone but new ones spring up. Old buildings are torn down and new ones built. Sure, Bridgeport does not have all the shopping and businesses it once did. There are no more theatres or bowling alleys, but there are still thriving businesses and restaurants. There are art galleries and other cultural gatherings. There are still churches and schools that are part of the fabric of Bridgeport. In other words – life still goes on in one of the older neighborhoods of Chicago.

It is interesting how some old sites look much better today while other sites have become decrepit or even have disappeared altogether. It is sad to see a place where several hundred people once worked and the place is now gone along with all the jobs. It is sad to see a theatre, where many generations gathered and grew up watching movies, now sit empty and boarded up. But who knows – maybe the building is about to start a new life after sitting empty for thirty years. In conclusion, this book will show the life of the past as well as the current life. And I think many will be amazed to see how Bridgeport has changed and continues to thrive after all these years!

This bath house was one of the last of its kind in Bridgeport. It was located at 2839 South Halsted. Bath houses were very important at one time in Chicago because of the lack of indoor plumbing in many houses. The photo was taken in 1960 right before the closing of this bath house.

The area today is the parking lot of a former heart clinic. Currently the property is for sale.

It was a well-known fact that immigrants found solace in churches and saloons. Bridgeport had a surplus of both! G.A. Ragon Saloon at 3459 South Halsted in the 1890's.

3459 South Halsted in 2015 - Both businesses help put you to sleep!

A very RARE photo of the Loomis theatre in 1936. The Loomis theatre was located at 2858 South Archer from 1913 until the 1950's and had about 300 seats. In 1936 Bridgeport had seven theatres.

2858 South Archer today. The Loomis theatre building and several blocks of businesses along south Archer met their demise with the construction of I-55 (The Stevenson Expressway) which is in the background.

Nativity church 1914
The church, founded in 1868 to meet the spiritual needs of the Irish, is one of the oldest churches in Chicago. Also, in the photo you can see Holden's Drug Store which was at this corner location for over 100 years!

Nativity church a hundred years later looking impressive. It is interesting that both structures in the photo from 1914 are still standing.

St. Mary's School in the 1950's

Today St. Mary's school is now De La Salle. The school is located on same block but with a new look.
De La Salle opened a high school for girls that replaced St. Mary's and Lourdes.
The house to the right looks about the same as the 1950's picture.

Bridgeport Restaurant around 1970.

Bridgeport restaurant today looking remarkably the same.

St. Anthony Church 1913

All Saints - St. Anthony Church today still going strong.

Pomierski Funeral Home at 32nd and Aberdeen in the 1920's.

Pomierski Funeral Home still serving the community at the same location almost one hundred years later.

Naps bowling alley in the 1970's

Naps was demolished about ten years ago. These new buildings were built in 2007 and are a mixed use of business and condos. Naps bowling was a part of Bridgeport for several decades and is sorely missed!

The Harmony Club in the 1970's, also known at the Lithuanian Dance Hall, stood at 3133 for many years. It was a dance hall that also had a four lane bowling alley. Because of numerous fights it was sometimes nicknamed the "bucket of blood".

The Harmony Club was torn down many years ago and today serves as a parking lot for the Pot Sticker House restaurant.

Holden School in 1907

Holden school over a hundred years later – still looking good! The school has about 600 students.

*Immaculate Conception Church at 3101 South Aberdeen in 1913
The church was built in 1911 for the increasing German population.*

Almost one hundred years later the church still stands and looks beautiful. It is now the Monastery of the Holy Cross. The monastery also is a bed and breakfast that allows people to pray with the monks. The building across street was a laundry mat for many years and is being rebuilt after a fire last year.

St. Bridget church in the 1950's. St. Bridget was located on Archer and also had a school. The church was the oldest in Bridgeport and was started by Irish immigrants in 1850. In its heyday in the 1940's and 1950's the church had 6000 parishioners. An interesting side note is that the Stevenson (I-55) had to be routed a bit differently than planned so that St. Bridget would not be torn down.

Sadly, St. Bridget was part of the massive Chicago diocese parish closings due to finances and was closed in 1990 to the dismay of many longtime parishioners. The long loved church met the wrecking ball in 1992. This new building was built in 2007 and is a senior residence home.

A very early photo of St. Bridget's Church taken in 1913.

A blast from the past – St. Bridget's hall.

*The Norwal theatre, which was right next to Naps bowling, was located at 518 West 26th street. It also had been the Butler theatre.
The Norwal, which had 280 seats, closed down in the 1950's.*

The Norwal theater location is now a newer building that houses condos and a law office.
The house from the old photo appears to be about the same.

Chicago street car turning from 31st street to Morgan Street in 1947. This line went to the Stockyards. The route and street car was discontinued in 1949.

The train tracks are gone but 68 years later there is still a liquor store at the same building! Caplan's or Kaplan's (note the sign differences!) is now Maria's liquor store which is a vibrant business.

Budrick Furniture Mar at 3411 South Halsted had a gorgeous facade. Budrik was a long time fixture in Bridgeport.

Today the building is the Chicago Boxing Club which offers boxing and personal training classes.

This building was the 26ᵗʰ Street Mennonite church at Union and 26ᵗʰ street. The church was built in the early 1900's and existed until the 1940's. After that it became a Catholic hall that hosted social events like dances.

The building is now over one hundred years old and still has many of the original features. Today it is used for apartments.

*The original Hickory Pit at Union and 28th in the 1950's.
The restaurant later moved to South Halsted where the Bridgeport Senior Suites are located. The Hickory Pit was known for their outstanding ribs. Alexander Greenburg, who was the head of the Canadian Ace Brewing company and had been long time friends in the past with Al Capone and Frank Nitti, was gunned down outside this restaurant on December 8, 1955 by two mobsters who were never found.*

The building still stands and is presently the St. Joseph Club.

Michalski Bakery was a bakery located at 3236 Racine street and was known for their Paczki (sort of a Polish doughnut).

Today the former bakery is a law office.

Mark White Park in the early 1900's. The field house at the right went along Halsted Street. The pool was located at the far right hand corner.

The same area along South Halsted today is now part of the ball fields. Mark White Park was changed to McGuane Park in the 1960's. The old field house was torn down and a new one built in the early 1970's.

The old swimming pool at Mark White/McGuane Park provided fun for many years.

The pool is a faded memory from long ago and is now ball diamond #2.
A new indoor pool was built with the new field house.

St. David's church and rectory in the 1930's.
The church had a unique look and was located in the 3200 block of Union Avenue.
Mayor Daley attended the Golden Jubilee Celebration in 1955.

St. David's was closed in 1995 after 90 years of existence. The former church site is now residential homes.

*Georges Café at the corner of 35th and Morgan Street in 1968.
The restaurant was at this site for many decades.*

Today the building is still a restaurant run by Johnny O's which has a long time Bridgeport association.

The original Johnny O's location at 828 West 31st in the early 1970's.

The old building was torn down a few years back and a nice looking new building with businesses and condos was built.

Raymond Baptist Church at 816 West 31st street in the mid 1960's.

Central Assembly of God is a church that still uses the building which was built in 1905.

The 400 block of West 26th street in 1966. Businesses included Mr. Christopher's restaurant, the Princess Shop, and Dalcamo Funeral Home.

Almost fifty years later Dalcamo is the only business left. The funeral home has expanded and been remodeled.

*Weller's department store at 32nd and Morgan in 1972.
Before Wellers the building was F & S Department store.*

Building looks about the same but Wellers is long gone. However, Co-Prosperity Sphere has brought life to the building again. Co-Prosperity is an experimental cultural center with a studio that hosts a variety of events such as art exhibits and music gatherings. There is even a radio station.

The 200 block of west 31st street in 1970. At the right is the Winery restaurant with service window on side. Also next to the Winery was the beloved Miss Val's dance studio where many people learned to dance.

Forty-five years later the Winery has been replaced by Rocky's Sports Restaurant while the other buildings are being renovated.

No matter where you lived in Bridgeport, no matter what side, no matter what parish or school, everybody remembers David's and the Governors Table restaurants. This picture was taken in 1972.

Gone! David's and the Governor Table location is now a parking lot and empty field adjacent to the new police station. A part of Bridgeport died the day that David's was destroyed by fire in 1980. The corner did come back to life in the 1980's when a Dunkin Donuts and laundromat were built where the restaurants once stood. But those newer buildings were torn down a few years ago when the new 9th District Police Station was built.
The city is looking to build new retail business in this location.

Ed's Snack Shop along with the Transit liquor store and a laundromat at the corner of West 31st and South Halsted in 1972. There were a few restaurants at this corner over the decades including Friars Open Kitchen.

In 2015 the corner building looks much the same as 43 years earlier. It is now a Cricket retail store. The liquor store is now occupied by a chiropractor office and a very busy Jiffy Lube now stands where the laundromat was. Central Assembly of God anchors the far left corner. Needless to say, this block is still very active.

The same picture but showing the Halsted side.
Notice there was a gas station next to Ed's snack shop.

Today the gas station has been replaced by several retail stores including a Foot Locker.

Atlas Uniform Company and its ramshackle building at 3130 South Halsted in 1972. The building to the far left is the Milda Hall.

The building has been replaced by the beautiful Deering (9th) district police station which was dedicated in 2008. The station is state of the art with over 44,000 square feet –much larger than the old 9th district building on South Lowe. The building cost $29 million to build.

A variety of small businesses existed at 33rd Place and Halsted in 1970.

The same block forty-five years later with a facelift and new businesses.

The 3500 block of South Halsted next to the Ramova theatre in 1954. Stores included Stella's Lingerie, Clara's Women Store and the Ramova Grill.

All the businesses are gone including the Ramova theatre. The Ramova Grill closed just a few years ago. Stella's and Clara's were long time businesses that lasted into the 1980's. There were a variety of businesses that used the buildings for several years after the stores closed. Everything was closed down a few years ago and currently the buildings are being renovated. Hopefully new life can come to these buildings in the near future.

A busy intersection at 35th and South Halsted in 1970. The 3400 block of South Halsted was a major shopping destination in Bridgeport for many decades.

Forty-five years later all new buildings and businesses make up the busy intersection!

The 3400 block of South Halsted in 1970. This block was loaded with stores and businesses. Included at different times was the Community Department Store, Kaplan Shoes, L & F Men's Wear, Normans Men & Boys store, Sally Ann Shop, Helen's Gift Shop, Bridgeport News, Rosa's Dress Shop and Burdeens Shoe store

Today there is an impressive new building anchoring the block. The building is a mixed use of housing and businesses. Some of the businesses include long time Bridgeport business Oscar's jewelry store, South Central Bank, Country Insurance, and Buffalo Wings and Rings restaurant. A physical therapy facility is also at the location.

The 700 block of West 31st street in 1966.
One of the businesses is the Blake and Lamb funeral home at 712.

The same block almost fifty years later. Overall the block looks a little better with new businesses. Blake and Lamb moved down the street to a very nice new facility.

Advance Cleaners and Progress Printing Company are a couple of the businesses seen in this 1972 photo of the 3300 block of South Halsted Street.

The 3300 block of South Halsted n 2015. Progress Printing is still at the location and going strong. The printing company has been in Bridgeport since 1933 and has done printing business for some of the biggest political figures in the city along with President Bill Clinton.

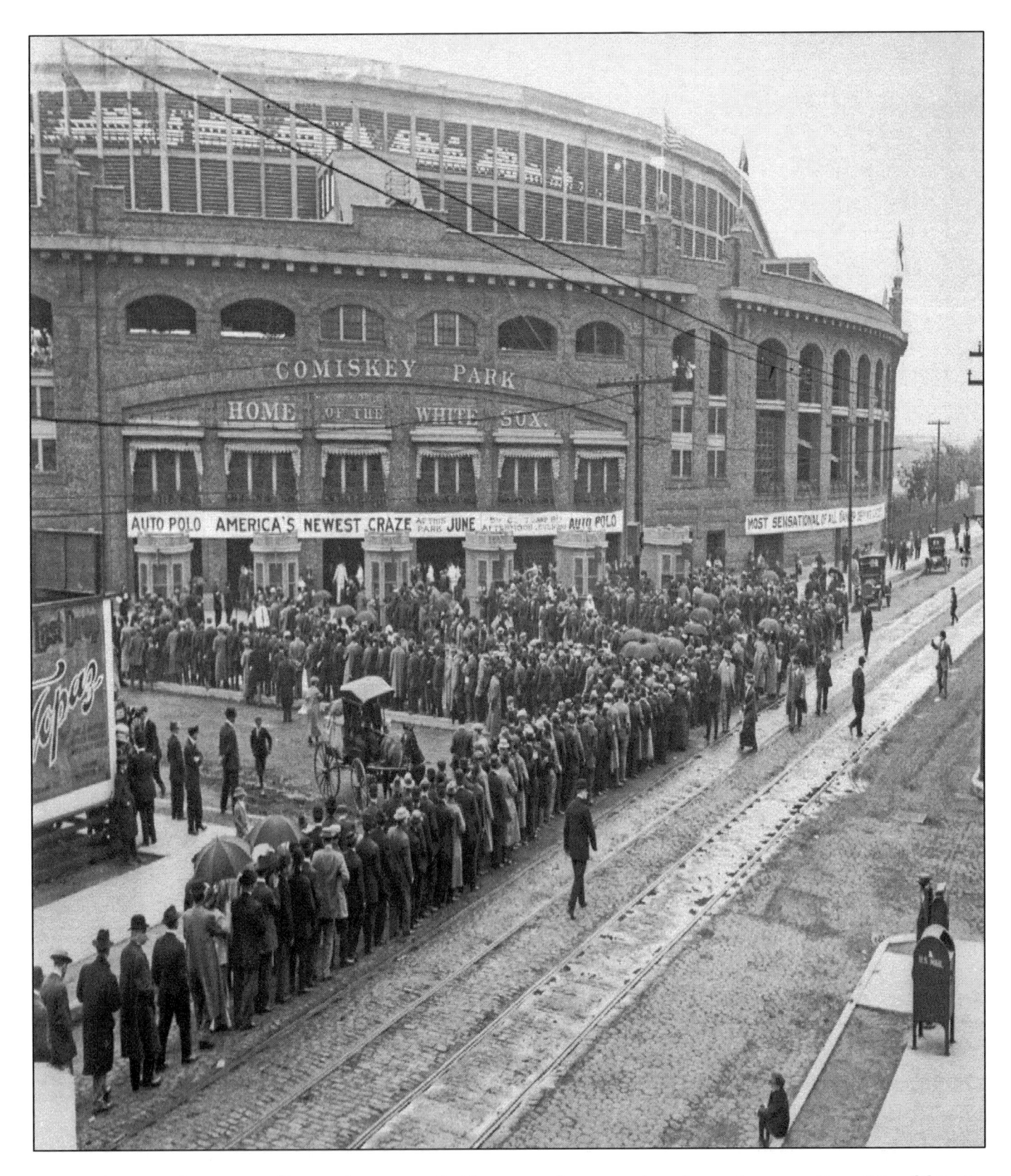

Comiskey Park in 1913. The stadium was built over a former city dump in 1910. Four World Series and three all-star games were played at Comiskey including the very first all-star game in 1933. Also, many of the Negro league all-star games were played at the park. The Chicago Cardinals football team played for several decades at Comiskey while the stadium hosted everything from boxing matches to rock concerts and roller derby. Among the many concerts performed was a Beatles concert in 1966.

The same spot today is a parking lot beside the new stadium.
The old Comiskey was demolished in 1991 and with it a lot of memories!

Comiskey Park was painted white in this 1980's shot.

The same spot thirty some years later – a lonely looking parking lot.

For many decades there was a Buick dealership at 907 West 35th street. It was first Milda Buick and then Morden Buick. Notice that gas at the Texaco station was just 33 cents! The building on the corner was a bar and apartment complex. Photo was taken in 1972.

The old Buick dealership building still is involved with cars with the Bridgeport Auto Body now using the site. Corner building is currently undergoing renovation.

Doremus Congregational Church in 1904. The church was located at 3033 South Normal and served the community until the 1990's.

There is still a church at the location with the façade looking similar from 111 years ago!
The church is now called New Life.

Ambrosia Brewing Company in 1953. The brewing company was located next to Schaller's Pump at 37th and South Halsted. At one time or another there were seven breweries in Bridgeport. This brewery was located at this spot since 1883 under various names including Southside Brewing Company, Fredrick Brothers and Junks Brewery. Ambrosia operated at this location for over twenty-five years and produced the well-known Nectar brand. Atlantic Brewing Company bought out Ambrosia in 1959.

It's hard to believe but the large plant today is a parking lot for Schaller's Pump.
The brewery after several years of losses, closed in 1965.

Right down the street from Ambrosia was perhaps Bridgeport's most famous brewery - the Manhattan Brewing Company which became Canadian Ace in 1947. The plant was located at 39th and Emerald. The plant was reported to have had mob connections with Frank Nitti owning part of the plant until his suicide in the early 1940's. The Canadian Ace brewery in Bridgeport became one of the biggest breweries in the country by the late 1940's. Lou Greenberg, mentioned elsewhere in this book, had been an owner of this plant when he was gunned down outside of the Hickory Pit restaurant at 28th and Union Street in 1955. This plant was the last brewery to operate in Bridgeport before closing down in the late 1960's.

All that remains today is an empty lot.

The Henn-Gabler Brewing Company in the early 1900's at 3400 South Racine (then it was called Centre Street).

The area today a very busy parking lot attached to the Bridgeport Art Center at 35th and Racine.

*The Ramova Theater and the 3500 block of South Halsted in 1984.
The Ramova was the last theatre to exist in Bridgeport. It was built in 1929 with a seating capacity of 1500 and was in existence until 1985. The last movie shown was Police Academy 2. Also included in shot are the local favorites Granata Bakery and Stella's clothing store. Both were long time businesses at the 3500 block location.*

All of the businesses are long gone in this current shot. The Ramova sign is still a very noticeable feature but the theatre has long been closed for almost thirty years. There has long been talk of what to do with the Ramova for many years but thus far nothing has come about. The Granata Bakery building is gone while all the businesses on the other side of the Ramova are shuttered. However, there is renovation work going on in all of the buildings. The MN business is a gallery and studio.

*Sonny's Barber Shop and two other businesses on
West 31st street and Morgan Street in 1972.*

Forty-three years later.

Lucille's Candy Store at Keeley and Lyman in 1965.
These type of small family owned corner stores were numerous in the Bridgeport area.

Same location fifty years later. No more candy!

A hardware and men's wear store at Bonfield and South Archer in 1978.

The building overall looks better today. The first floor business is a Tae Kwon Do business while the upper floors are apartments.

The corner of Throop, Archer and Fuller Street in the 1960's. St. Bridget is to the left.

While part of the corner building remains, the rest of the block has undergone a massive change with new buildings.

A picture of the R.V. Kunka's drugstore at 2899 South Archer in 1978.
The building façade with Kunka, Ice Cream and Drugs signature was made in the 1930's.
The building itself like many South Archer buildings was built in the late 1800's.

The buildings are still there but Kunka's has been closed since 2009. The old school tile fronted deco façade from the 1930's with Kunka on it is still intact and in good condition. Kunka's was one of the last neighborhood drug stores in the Bridgeport area. Sadly the neighborhood drug stores have been replaced by big national drug store chains. Kunka's drug store was part of the community for at least 75 years.

St. George's church in 1984.
The church was located at 33rd and Lituanica. St. George's was built in 1902 and was one of the first Lithuanian churches built in America and was one of the largest.

The church was closed and torn down in 1993 and is now a playground and parking lot for Armour school. The school building in the background is still in use by Armour school. An interesting side note is that many furnishings from St. George's interior was shipped back to Lithuania.

A corner grocery store at 3428 South Lituanica in 1971.

The store is now a residence. There was a time when it seemed that every other block had a corner grocery store. Though many have disappeared there are still several operating in the Bridgeport area.

A photo taken in 1961 of a corner tavern at 33rd and Lituanica that was catty corner to St. George.

The site today is private residences.

The District National Bank was a long time bank on West 35th street. Photo is from 1968.

District National Bank changed names including recently Chicago Community Bank. It is now Byline Bank. The building still looks good and has kept many of its features over the years.

Milda Hall at 3140 South Halsted in 1972. Milda Hall had just about everything in its long history. Milda opened as the Milda Theatre in 1914 and was one of the larger movie houses in Bridgeport for several decades with seating for 900. It also hosted wrestling and boxing matches for years as well as being a banquet hall.

The site today is part of the new 9th district police station.

Ricobene's Original Stand in 1946.

Ricobene's Restaurant 2015

The 200 block of West 26th street in 1966. The Wells Street Tavern is in the middle while the Ricobene's stand is to its left with the Italian American club at far left.

In 2015 several of the buildings look similar. Ricobene's has grown and expanded into full fledge restaurant. The Italian-American club has moved to a very nice facility on Shields avenue. But the original building still stands and hosts a few small businesses.

Bernie's Groceries at Wallace and 32nd street in 1966.

Almost fifty years later the area seems a bit desolate.

*All Saints church at Wallace and 25th street in 1973.
The church closed in 1968 and merged with St. Anthony's at 28th and Wallace.
That church is called All Saints-St. Anthony.*

Today the former church site is an apartment complex.

Street car 3096 would go from Archer down Throop to Farrell Street and onto Morgan Street. The line would then go to the stockyards. This photo was taken in 1947 at Farrell and 31st street.

Farrell and 31st street today. The 3096 street car and route was discontinued in 1949.

The corner of 35th and Morgan Street in 1938. The two-story Spiegel building had just been built. A few years later they would add two more floors to the building.
The gas station on the corner was selling gas for SEVENTEEN cents!
Notice the beautiful brick streets along with street car rails.

In 2015 the Spiegel's building is still standing but Spiegel's long ago packed up and moved out. The building is currently being renovated. The gas station has been gone for a few decades. Most recently is was a fast food restaurant. The building is empty and being renovated.

*Joslyn manufacturing plant at 3700 South Morgan Street in 1939.
The company was established in 1902.*

The plant was in operation until a few years ago when it closed down.
The plant and building, along with hundreds of jobs are gone now.

Larsen and Son hardware store and Schaller's Pump in 1971.

The building and business no longer exist.

The Marion Theatre around 1914.
The Marion was one of the first theatres in Bridgeport and was a nickelodeon theatre that showed silent films. The two features in the above picture were The Escape of Jim Dolan and The Massacre. The theatre was located around 3446-48 South Halsted.

The theatre location today is part of new building complex built at 35th and South Halsted.

McGuane Park playground in the early 1980's.

The current McGuane park playground at same location. It would seem that the playground looks more fun now!

The 3300 hundred block of South Halsted between 33rd place and 34th Street in the 1960's. Two liquor stores and Malelo Camera Shop.

The same block in 2015. The liquor stores have been replaced by a health center (might be good thing!) and a tire repair shop. Malelo Camera Shop is still anchoring the corner.
Malelo's has been in business since 1950 and is one of the older businesses in Bridgeport.

The 9th District (Deering) police station at 35th and Lowe in the 1960's. Notice the cool looking police car. The station was built in 1938.

The old 9th boarded up and empty.

The 9th District moved to a spacious new complex at 31st and South Halsted in 2012. Fire station 29 next door is still used by the Chicago Fire Department. If those old walls could talk they would surely have many tales to tell!

Archer and Bonfield looking west in the early 1900's. You can see St. Bridget in the distance. South Archer Avenue was a major business district from the early 1900's through the 1950's. The business district waned and part of it even disappeared when the Stevenson expressway was put in.

The same corner nearly 100 years later. Though South Archer is not what it was in the early to mid-1950's, there are still many thriving businesses and restaurants that dot the landscape.

The Rexall Union Drug Store at 3501 South Halsted in the 1930's.

The same building is used today by Chase bank. It is very interesting that the building to the left on 35th street (three story white building) almost looks exactly the same as eighty years ago!

The corner of Archer and Halsted in 1963.
The building included the Point Lounge and other businesses.

Today the building has made way for a thriving Citgo gas station along with Dunkin Donuts and Baskin Robbins.

The Lewis Pharmacy located at 2822 South Archer in the 1950's. The street next to the pharmacy is Farrell. If you notice you will see big oil tank in the background that was along the Chicago River.

The exact same location today. The Stevenson expressway (first called Southwest expressway) was finished in 1964 and wiped out several blocks along South Archer including the 2800 block. Even the street next to the pharmacy (Farrell) was taken out. All the buildings, including the oil tank, are gone. Lewis Pharmacy relocated across the street at 2833 and survived into the 1970's.

Sterns Quarry in the 1960's.
The quarry operated from 1830 until 1970. Much of the limestone dug from Sterns Quarry was used to construct downtown buildings and city roadways.

Today Sterns Quarry has been turned into an incredible inner city park. Harry Palmisano Park is across the street from McGuane Park and has 27 acres including a fishing pond in the lower left hand corner. There are walking tracks as well as sledding hill. Sterns Quarry at one point was excavated down to 380 feet. After closing the quarry was slowly filled in over forty years by city with construction street waste. The park was built upon the landfill and opened in 2009 and has been enjoyed by thousands.

The fishing pond and nature walk at Palmisano Park.

People enjoying sledding at Palmisano Park.

A close up of Granata Bakery in 1984. People loved their Italian bread!

Today there is an empty lot where Granata once stood.

The Ramova Grill at 3510 South Halsted was established in 1929. The restaurant was a longtime favorite among locals. The place was known for their homemade chili. The blurry photo is from the 1970's.

Co-owners Tony Dinos and Bob Gertos worked at the Ramova Grill for fifty-two years. The well-loved eatery was closed in 2012 after 83 years in business – thus ending a Bridgeport landmark.
The building now is being renovated for new business.

Art's hot dog stand at 31st and Morgan Street in 1970.

Today, Pleasant House is doing a thriving business at the location.
Pleasant House is known for meat and vegetarian pies.

Holden drug store was a long time fixture for over one hundred years at 3659 South Union.

The Holden drug store or Apothecary lasted into the 2000's but eventually went by the wayside. It too was a Bridgeport landmark. Interestingly the mail box is still in the exact location!

A blurry ad for Tortoriello Funeral home located at 3007 South Union. There were a lot of small neighborhood funeral homes in Bridgeport back in the day and now only a few remain.

Today the funeral home is a private residence.

The Wrigley factory at 35th and Ashland in the 1940's. The plant was built in 1911.

The plant was the last Wrigley plant in Chicago and closed in 2006. Many folks from Bridgeport found employment at this plant which at one time employed 1600 people. At time of closing over 500 people worked at the plant. The building is now slowly being demolished. There are rumors of a big shopping center replacing the buildings and surrounding land.

Healthy Foods restaurant at 3236 South Halsted was a long time restaurant favorite of local Bridgeporters. The bustling Lithuanian restaurant started in the Bridgeport area in the 1930's.

Healthy Food closed in 2009. The building is in the process of being renovated.

COOL EXTRA STUFF

The Bridgeport Bakery has been at this Archer location for over 80 years.
They are well known for their Paczki's on Fat Tuesday each year.

This building at 622 West 31st street housed the Wallace Theatre which existed from 1912 to 1966.

This building at 3307 South Lituanica was for many years Phillips Funeral Home.

P. O'Neills located at 33rd Street and South Halsted in the 1890's.

St. Bridget's Rectory still stands and is now a private residence.

The new park was built across from the old stadium and is now called U.S. Cellular Field – MERCY!

The Mark White/McGuane Park pool sitting empty – photo date unknown.

Cool photo of Sterns Quarry in 1965.

The Morgan street trolley nearing 35th and Morgan Street in the 1930's. George's Café is to right and Standard service station to the left. Both businesses are featured in the book.
One can also see a barbershop as well as the brick streets.

Though All Saints Church met the wrecking ball, the school across the street still survives today as apartments.

This building at 3335 South Halsted was the Universal shoe store back in the 1960's and 1970's.
The fading vestiges of a long ago sign announces "Shoes for the entire family".
The business today is Hardscrabble Gifts which happens to sell Bridgeport stuff.

The building at 3337 South Morgan was the long time Bridgeport Pharmacy. It was opened at this location by Hattie Lescauska in 1922. The pharmacy was still at this lcoation in the 1970's.

This building at 3310-12 South Morgan was the National Ballroom for many years going back to the 1930's. National Ballroom would hold dances and muisc gatherings.

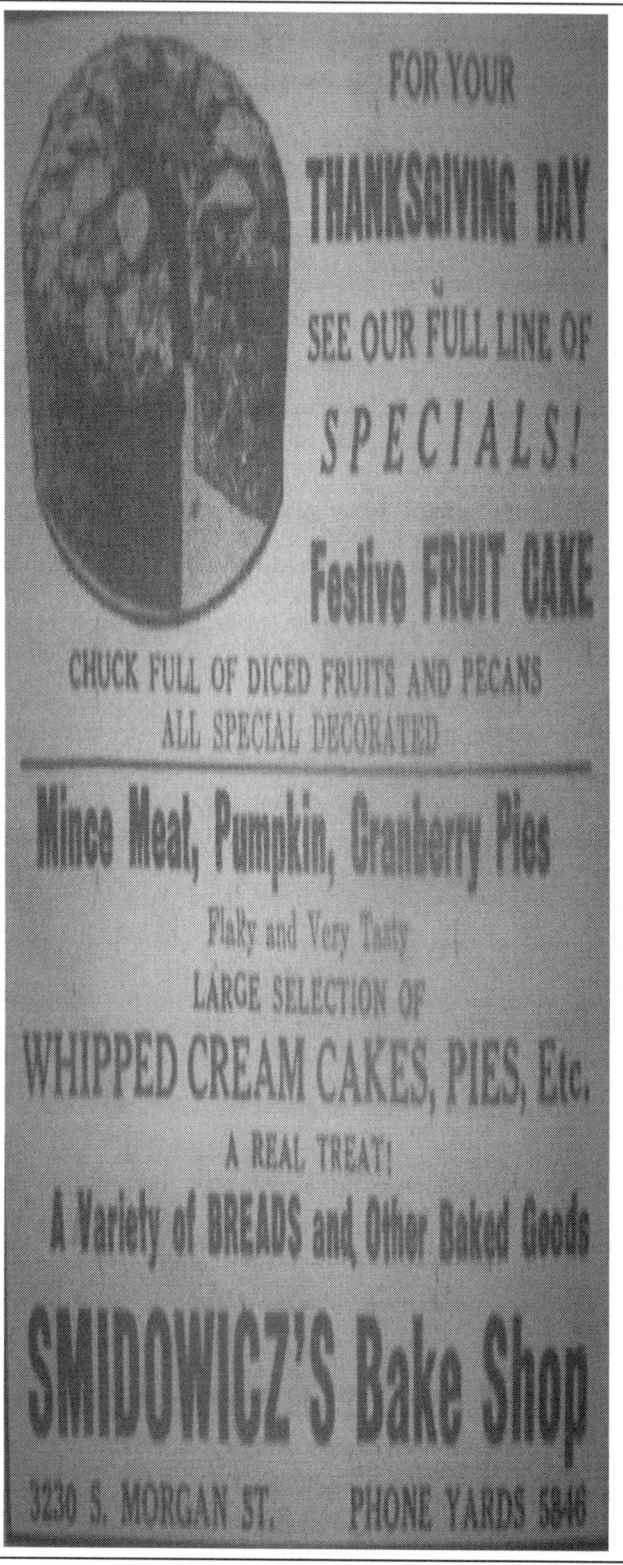

This non decript building at 3320 South Morgan next to the Polo Café was once the home of Smidowicz Bake Shop back in the 1930's and 1940's.

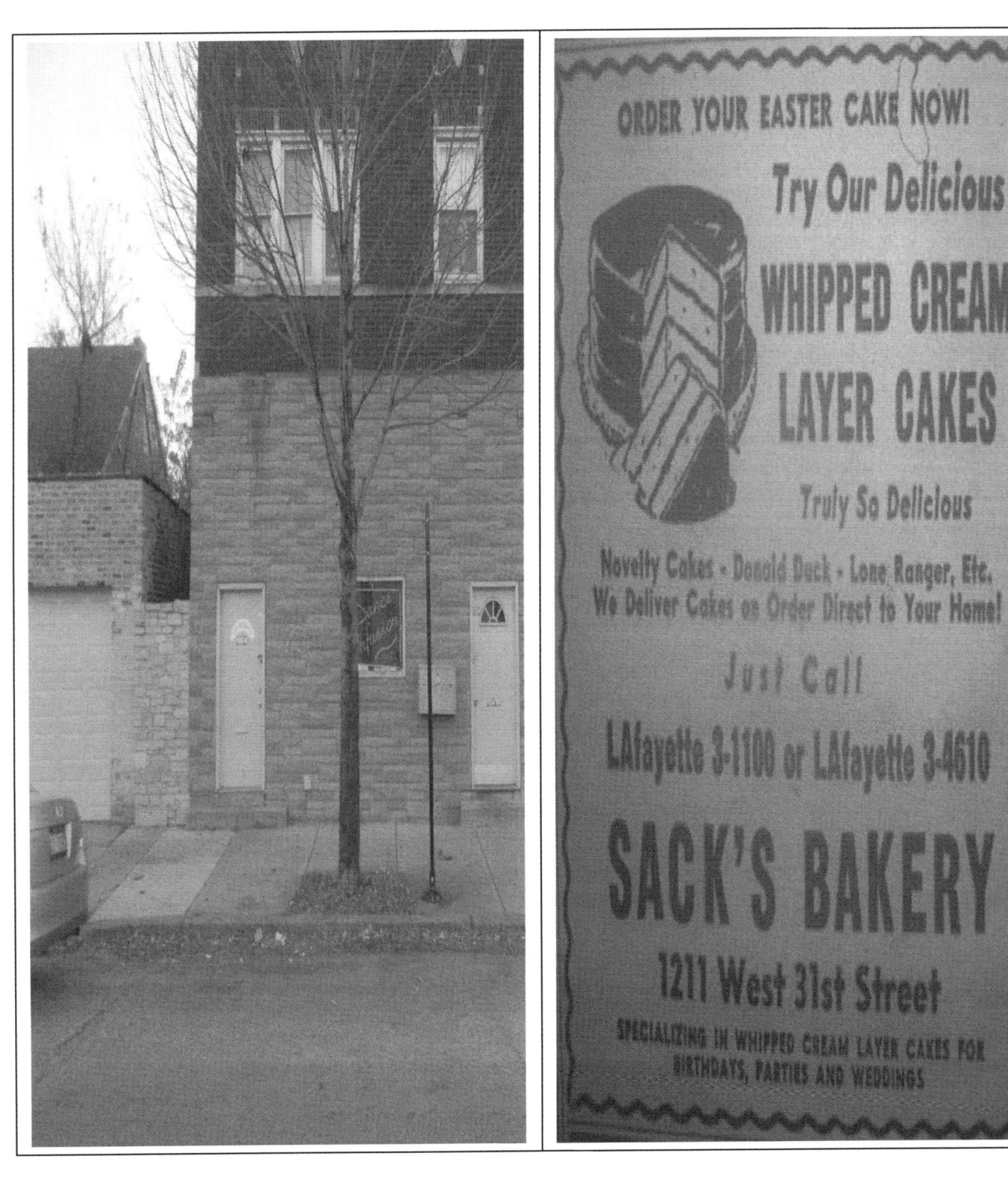

This building at 1211 West 31st street was for many years Sack's Bakery going back to the 1930's.

This location at 3254-56 South Wallace was for several decades Dressel's Bakery. The bakery was really known for their cakes, especially the chocolate fudge whipped cream cake! The Dressel family started the bakery at this location in 1913. By the 1920's the crowds were so large on Saturdays as they lined the sidewalks that the police had to come and help with crowd control. In the 1940's they were baking 10,000 cakes a week and had to install ten phone lines to keep up with orders. Dressel's branched out to another location in Cicero while building a plant at 66th and Ashland. Many people are surprised to learn that Dressel's was bought by a national company back in the 1960's and that their cakes were sold on a national level. Altogether, Dressel's was in Bridgeport for over eighty years and finally disappeared in the 1990's.

St. Bridget's Church
2928 ARCHER AVENUE

MASSES EASTER SUNDAY

6:00, 8:00, 10:30, 12:00 Noon

HOLY THURSDAY
Low Mass 8:00 A.M. For Mothers and Children
Mass 6:30 P.M.
GOOD FRIDAY
Adoration of Blessed Sacrament
7:00 A.M. to 3:00 P.M.
& Solemn Liturgy 3:00 P.M.
HOLY COMMUNION
Stations of the Cross & Sermon 7:30 P.M.
HOLY SATURDAY
Ceremonies Begin at 7 P.M. Followed by the Easter Vigil Mass

REVEREND WALTER H. CHELMINSKI
REVEREND ROBERT PELTON

LOOMIS
EDMUD LOWE IN
GIRL ON THE FRONT PAGE
HEADLINES OF 25 YEARS

NOR-WAL

FREE! FREE! To The Ladies
MET-ROSE TREND DINNERWARE
Every Tues., Wed., Thurs., Mar. 7-8-9

DON'T MISS THIS NEW SENSATIONAL SMART DINNERWARE ... NEVER BEFORE GIVEN AWAY IN ANY THEATRE. ITS NEW STYLE SHAPE WILL THRILL YOU! (NOT AN OLD FASHIONED ANTIQUE DESIGN) ... BUT MODERN AS TODAY! ... ITS HERE AT THE

LOOMIS THEATRE ONLY!

Nobody Can Offer You This Beautiful Dinnerware
FOR SO LITTLE MONEY!

ADULTS, 35c   CHILDREN, 14c Tax Inc.

LOOMIS THEATRE
2858 Archer Ave.
(A small service charge added for handling)

NORWAL THEATRE
518 W. 26th St.

Completely Reconditioned

FRIDAY AND SATURDAY - SEPTEMBER 20-21
"DRAGONWYCK"

SUNDAY AND MONDAY - SEPTEMBER 22-23
"PERILOUS HOLIDAY"
"THE RUNAROUND"

TUESDAY - SEPTEMBER 24 — ONE DAY ONLY
"THE PAYOFF"
"HOW DO YOU DO?"

WEDNESDAY AND THURSDAY - SEPTEMBER 25-26
"TERROR BY NIGHT"
"OUR HEARTS WERE YOUNG AND GAY"

The exterior and sign for Milda Hall theatre in the 1920's.

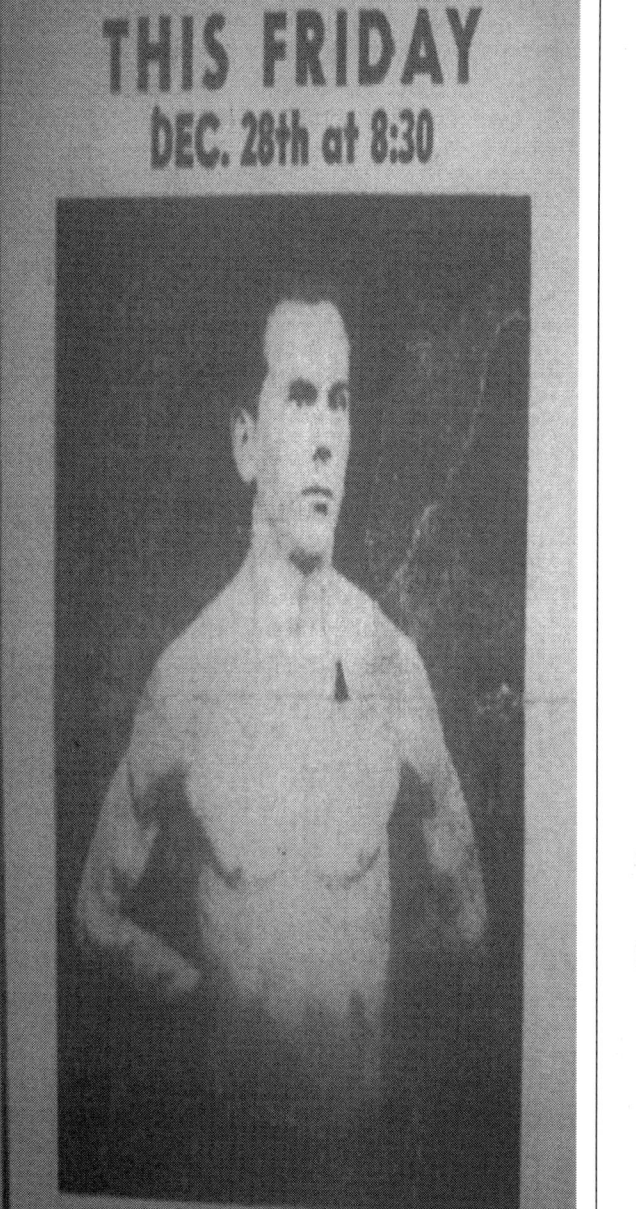

MILDA
3140 So. Halsted St.
Telephone Victory 4424

SUNDAY and MONDAY, MARCH 1 and 2
Bing! It's Bing Again, Singing His Heart Awa

"TWO FOR TONIGHT"

YOU'LL GET A BANG OUT OF BING!

Bing CROSBY
Joan BENNETT
Mary Boland
Lynne Overman
Thelma Todd

Down to his last grand (piano), Bing pursues the even tenor of his ways, also a brace of bee-utiful blondes. And does he make good! The sweethearts of "Mississippi" in a new success.

ANDY CLYDE COMEDY RIOT "HOT PAPRIK
COLOR CARTOON   News

WRESTLING
THIS FRIDAY
DEC. 28th at 8:30

MILDA ARENA
3140 S. HALSTED STREET

The inside of the Ramova Grill.

Inside of the Ramova Theatre.

FRIDAY and SATURDAY
MAY 22 and 23

A Girl of the Wilderness and a Man of the World

SYLVIA SIDNEY
FRED MacMURRAY
HENRY FONDA
in
"THE TRAIL OF THE LONESOME PINE"

A Blazing Love Story of the Feud-Torn Kentucky Hills

FILMED IN NATURAL COLOR

FRED STONE - SPANKY McFARLAND

—ADDED—
JACKIE COOGAN in "LOVE IN SEPTEMBER"
Cartoon - News - Oddity "Primitive Pitcairn"

Play SCREENO Saturday

$50.00 CASH PRIZES — ?-$ CASH POT $-?

RAMOVA
35th. AND HALSTED

Telephone YARDS 5957
HOME OF THE LATEST AND BEST PICTURES
Watch For Our Ads in Daily Papers

SUN., MON. and TUES., MAY 17, 18 and 19

THE GREATEST ENTERTAINER OF ALL TIMES

The One and Only
CHARLIE CHAPLIN in "MODERN TIMES"

No One in the World Can Make You Laugh as Heartily or Touch Your Heart as Deeply

RAMOVA
HUMPHREY BOGART IN
THE CAINE MUTINY
AND CHARGE
OF THE LANCERS
RAMOVA
ENJOY THE LATEST AND BEST OF HITS
ON OUR GIANT PANORAMIC SCREEN

Chicago Daily Tribune

PUPIL SLAIN IN GANG BATTLE

Police Charge Teen-Agers with Murder in Gang Warfare

ung hoodlums in police custody yesterday after being d with murder in fatal shooting of Kenneth Sleboda at d Morgan sts. during fight between rival gangs. They are (left to right): Eugene O'Brien, Raymond Kennedy, J. Maher, Gerald Walsh, Larry Degnan, James Sarna, and Jan Bartlett.

The Gang Murder in Bridgeport that Made National News

On a hot evening July 1, 1955, Kenneth Sleboda, who lived at 32nd and May, had gotten off work and stopped off at Chick's Chili at 3208 South Morgan to get a soda pop. Sleboda, who was going to be a senior at De LaSalle in the fall, came out of the shop and stopped to talk to several kids hanging out. Just then three car loads of teens drove up and mayhem broke out. The teens jumped out of the cars with chains and baseball bats and attacked the group. Some ran while others were beaten. In the midst of the chaos a shot gun blast came from one of the cars. At that moment Sleboda fell to his knee and then collapsed. The group ran back to their cars and took off. The attack has just taken a few minute. But on that hot night long ago, Kenneth Sleboda, who was not in any gang and by all accounts a nice kid, took his last breath and died from the gunshot wound. His funeral would be held at St. Mary's.

Later the gang would say the beatings were revenge for a member who had gone with his girlfriend to St. Mary's carnival and had been beaten by neighborhood toughs. Some of the gang members were from the 38th street area of Union and Lowe while others came from surrounding neighborhoods. It's interesting to note that a few of the kids were also De LaSalle Students. The killing and attack made the front page of the Chicago Tribune while also making national news. Chicago, New York and other cities were experiencing an explosion of gangs and gang related troubles. This story fit the narrative of the current concern. Clement Macis, who was only fourteen at the time, claimed the gun went off accidently. He was sentenced to fifteen years in prison while several of his gang mates received shorter sentences. This incident shows that even sixty years ago gangs were a source of trouble in the city of Chicago and even Bridgeport!

3208 South Morgan Street is a parking lot for Pulaski Savings today.

'Revenge' Called Motive

Murder charges were placed late yesterday against eight of 13 rowdies who figured Friday night in what prosecutors said was the "senseless murder" of Kenneth Sieboda, 17. The other five were turned over to juvenile authorities to await grand jury action.

The charges were made after members of the gang told with indifference of the events which led to the shooting. Clement Macis, 14, of 3841 Union av., who fired the 12 gauge shotgun blast which killed Sieboda, asserted the shooting was "an accident."

He was one of the five placed in custody of juvenile authorities.

His companions told of their assault on Sieboda and several others at 32d and Morgan sts. Most of the prisoners smoked cigarets and leaned against desks or walls while awaiting interrogation.

Faces Murder Charge

Assistant State's Attorneys Frank Ferlic and Frank Whelan predicted that Macis, a pupil in Tilden Technical High school, who has been working as a crate handler during the summer, also would be charged with murder.

Sieboda, of 3213 May st., a senior in De La Salle High school, died within a few minutes after the shotgun charge struck him in the side. The murder weapon, which Macis had taken from home without the knowledge of his father, Stanley, 37, had been "test fired" in Saber's field, 37th st. and Lithuanica av., by a member of the gang a short time before the shooting.

Revenge Held Motive

The motive for the attack was revenge for a beating suffered last Sunday by a member of the gang, Eugene O'Brien, 17, of 932 W. 52d st., a pupil in De La Salle High school. O'Brien said he met a girl at a church carnival and was assaulted later by three men while walking the girl to her home.

End Notes

Photo Credits

Chicago Historical Society (photos rights paid)

Pages 4, 6, 12, 14, 18, 22, 24, 28, 30, 50, 52, 54, 56, 58, 60, 62, 64, 68, 70 72, 74, 78, 80, 82, 84, 86, 90, 92, 94, 96, 98, 100, 102,104, 106, 108, 110, 112, 114, 116, 118, 120, 122, 124, 128, 130, 132, 134, 138, 140, 154, 156, 158, 162, 134, 136, 172, 174, 193

University of Minnesota (photos rights paid)
Pages 36, 38, 144

Chicago Transit Authority (permission granted)
Pages 34, 124

Chicago Park District (permission granted)
Pages 44-46-136,150, 176-177

Cinema Treasures (photo rights paid)
Pages 8, 186, 188, 191

University of Illinois Chicago (photos rights paid)
Pages 146, 148

Chicago Diocese (permission granted)
Pages 10,16, 26, 48, 90

Private Photos (permission granted)
Pages 20, 32, 40, 42

Site Design Group (permission granted)
Pages 151, 153

Trolley Dodger (permission granted)
Page 177

Newberry Library (permission granted)
Pages 10, 16, 26

Bridgeport News (permission granted)
170, 182-187, 189

Publication Preparation
Ginny Caponigro

****

Bridgeport Then and Now

And other available titles

Bridgeport Memories Volume One

Bridgeport Memories Volume Two

Available through
Central Assembly of God
816 W. 31st
Chicago, Il 60608
312-326-1818

centralassembly@rocketmail.com

We are always looking for new photos.

If you have any old photos of Bridgeport (buildings, streets, etc.) that you would like to share with us, please feel free to send us a scanned copy or contact us for more information.

****

Made in the USA
Charleston, SC
30 November 2015